SUPER SMART SEEDS

By Tom Hooke

Published by New Generation Publishing in 2016

First Edition

ISBN: 978-1-78719-259-1

www.newgeneration-publishing.com

New Generation Publishing

This book belongs to

_____

Dedicated to my darling wife & chief advisor
Barbara & to my mother, the artist Susan Morland.

The story of Coconut seed - via Water

'Where are you going Coconut in your tough as a nut shell?' Sunny the sun asks.

'To seek a home.'

Sunny wants to know more.' Where is home Coconut?'

'I can float like a boat. So it is wherever the sea takes me. It could be miles and miles away.' Coconut says, thinking Sunny asks a lot of questions.

'Good luck Coconut.' Says Sunny, seeing Coconut bobbing in the water & thinking it funny.

3

'Welcome to your new home Coconut.' Sunny says, amazed at how far Coconut has floated.

'Thank you Sunny. Do you know where I am?'

'I spy you on an island in the middle of the Indian ocean with what might be a monkey for company.' Sunny replies. Sunny is pleased to see some of Coconut's distant relatives already there, so Coconut will not be lonely & despair.

'Clipity clop! Now I can grow tall & sway in the breeze & make new coconuts to drop.'

The story of Dandelion seed - via Wind

'Where are you going Dandelion in all your finery?' Sunny asks.

'To seek a home.'

Where is home Dandelion?' Sunny does like to know a lot.

'Wherever the wind takes me. You see I am so light just a shiver of wind will help me to take flight. It could be miles & miles away!'

'Good luck Dandelion.' Says Sunny, thinking Dandelion will certainly need lots of luck as well as lots of pluck.

'Welcome Dandelion to your new home.' Sunny says, amazed at how far Dandelion has blown.

'Thank you Sunny. Do you know where I am?' Replies Dandelion, wondering how Sunny seems to be everywhere all at the same time.

'You are in a field full of wild flowers like Campion, Vetch & Marigold. Oh & look there are Daisy & Maisy two very friendly cows.' Sunny is happy Dandelion will have so many new colourful friends.

'Dandy doo what a flight! And most importantly I am alright. Now I can grow green, yellow & beautiful.' Dandelion is very happy.

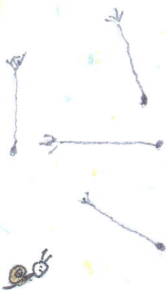

The story of Sycamore seed - via Twirling

Where are you going Sycamore seed with your fancy wings?' Sunny sings.

'To seek a home.'

'Where is home Sycamore?' Sunny always wants to know more.

'Wherever my wings take me. It could be miles & miles away!' Sycamore says, already feeling giddy with going up & down & round & round.

'Good luck Sycamore.' Sunny calls as Sycamore whizzes round faster & faster making Sunny feel dizzier & dizzier.

11

'Welcome to your new home Sycamore.' Says Sunny, surprised at how far Sycamore has whirled & twirled.

'Thank you Sunny. Do you know where I am?' Sycamore no longer feels giddy & instead feels really quite calm.

'You are in a crack in the ground on an old factory site full of all sorts of rusty & crusty things.' Sunny replies not at all sure it looked very nice for Sycamore, even with a rat called Rattus Rattus for company.

'Greaty great what a twirl! Now I can grow into a huge tree & make this place a lovely space.'

13

The story of Strawberry seed - via Bird

'Where are you going Strawberry seed on your magnificent red carriage?' Sunny wants to know.

'To find a home.' Says Strawberry, pleased with the praise & only a little nervous at being so high in the sky.

'Where is home Strawberry?' As ever one question is never enough for Sunny.

'After this bird has made a meal of me it will be wherever this bird's wings takes me. It could be miles & miles away!'

'Good luck Strawberry.' Says Sunny, not at all sure being eaten by a bird is the very best way to find a home.

'Welcome to your new home Strawberry. Though I have to say you are in a bit of a mess.' Sunny is not easy to impress.

'Thank you Sunny. Do not worry about the mess it will help me grow. Do you know where I am, please show?'

'You are being watched by a kangaroo, who is in hiding, having escaped from a zoo. In a wood with dappled light.' Sunny says with delight.

'Yummy yum what a sensation. Now I can grow lots more Strawberries for your delectation!'

The story of Sweet Pea seed - via Explosion

'Where are you going Sweet Pea so fast & furious?' Sunny is as ever so very curious.

'To find a home.'

'Where is home Sweet Pea?' Sunny asks, startled at Sweet Pea seed moving at such explosive speed.

'Wherever I fall down. It could be miles & miles away.'

'Good luck Sweet Pea.' Says Sunny, sorry that Sweet Pea might be going too fast to see & might become lost & all at sea.

'Welcome to your new home Sweet Pea.' Sunny says, pleased Sweet Pea is not lost, hurt or at sea.

'Thank you Sunny. Do you know where I am?'

'Luckily for you, by a hedgerow with a pleasant pheasant for company, so from small you can grow tall.' Sunny says with delight.

'Wriggly & climbly what a blast! Soon I will be many colours & gorgeous at last.'

The story of Poppy seed - via Scattering

'Where are you going Poppy, so tiny & so many?' Sunny asks as sweet as honey.

'To find a home.'

'Where is home Poppy?'

'Wherever the scattering takes me. It could be miles & miles away!' Poppy is feeling a little out of control but is happy to be out & on a roll.

'Good luck Poppy.' Sunny is amazed & dazed by how many scattered seeds of Poppy there are.

2.

'Welcome to your new home Poppy.' Sunny calls, noticing that Poppy after all has not gone too far at all.

'Thank you Sunny. Do you know where I am?' Poppy is still a little confused because of all that scattering & rattling.

'Really Poppy! Just look around you. You have not gone far. And look, what a happy chance, two hares have come out to dance.' Sunny is surprised Poppy has not realised where Poppy is, but can see Poppy is as happy as Poppy is.

'Bippy bop rattle the pod! Now I can start growing in my thousands & thousands.'

The story of Peanut seed - via Self Planting

'Where are you going Peanut in your lightweight brown pod?' Sunny demands to know.

'To find a home.'

'Where is home?' Says Sunny nosey as ever.

'Wherever I am right now. I plant myself.' Peanut replies with a smile.

'Good for you.' For once Sunny did not say good luck because Peanut knows exactly where to go & needs no luck.

'Welcome home Peanut. I must say you did not have far to go.'

'Where is home?' Peanut says & then laughs. 'Tee hee, only kidding. Home is where home is.'

'Ha, Ha, tee hee! Oh, & look, you are being watched by two hyenas called Zach & Zeldo.' For once Sunny is not worried and also finds it funny.

'Plipity plop how hilarious! All I do is stay put to plant to grow more Peanuts.'

The story of Hazelnut seed - via Squirrel

'Where are you going Hazelnut in your very hard shell shaped a little like a bell?' Sunny asks.

'To find a home.'

'Where is home?' Sunny as ever wants to know.

'Wherever this squirrel buries me. It could be here it could be there but personally I hope it is near.' Hazelnut says, feeling Squirrel's sharp claws gripping.

'Good luck Hazelnut.' Sunny says hoping Hazelnut arrives soon & not too scratched.

31

'Welcome to your new home Hazelnut.' Sunny says. 'I can just see you under the earth so snug just like being under a rug.'

'Thank you Sunny. Do you know where I am?' Says Hazelnut smiling & feeling nice and warm & cosy.

'In a wood not too far away where you can grow tall & sway & soon be covered in nuts with which squirrels can play.'

'Nutty nuts! I will grow & produce more nuts which squirrels can sow all in a row.

The story of Tumbleweed seed - via tumbling

'Where are you going Tumbleweed so scratchy & round & light but strong?'

'To find a home.'

'Where is home Tumbleweed?' Sunny asks because it was far from obvious how this could work.

'Wherever the blowy winds tumbles me. It could be miles & miles away.' Tumbleweed is feeling giddy with all this rolling around & feels it would be a boon to stop soon.

'Good luck Tumbleweed.' Says Sunny seeing Tumbleweed is getting bruised and not amused.

35

'Welcome to your new home Tumbleweed.' Says Sunny seeing Tumbleweed hiding in all sorts of places and funny spaces.

'Thank you Sunny. Do you know where I am?'

'You are scattered all around & about under the bright blue sky. So many seeds to make more Tumbleweeds.'

'Roly poly! What a rumble & a tumble & a jumble! Now I can make roots & shoots & be beautiful again in all sorts of spaces & funny places.'

The story of Burdock seed - via Clinging

'Where are you going to Burdock?' Sunny asks.

'To find some fur & then a home & by the way I am also called a burr.'

'Where is home Burdock?' Sunny asks, finding Burdock hard to spot on the spotty dog.

'Wherever this dog takes me. It could be miles & miles away!' Burdock is quite enjoying the ride, happy to be a Burr on a dog rather than on a bear or a hedgehog.

'Good luck Burdock.' Sunny says looking at all Burdock's hooks and wonders how Burdock will ever reach the ground & be found.

'Welcome to your new home Burdock.' Says Sunny a little worried Burdock might have been hurt after being scratched from dog to dirt.

'Thank you Sunny. Do you know where I am?'

'By a stream where the dog ran out of steam & in a field where two moles are politely chatting.'

'Burr, burr b burry burr!' Burdock sings merrily, so happy to be in a place so safe with plenty of space.

41

The story of Cornflower seed - via Crawling

'Where are you going Cornflower?' Sunny asks.

'To find a home.'

'Where is home?' Sunny wants to know.

'Wherever I can crawl. It will not be far.' Is Cornflower's reply said with a sigh. This sigh in Cornflower's reply is because it is very difficult for a little seed to crawl over ground so rough & so tough.

'Good luck Cornflower. It looks very difficult & quite a feat to move with no feet.' Says Sunny.

43

'Welcome to your new home Cornflower.' Says Sunny.

'Thank you Sunny. I know I have not travelled far but far enough is good enough for me. Do you know where I am?'

'In the same meadow just a little further along so all is right and nothing is wrong. You have for company a badger all of a puzzled & in wonder at how you got here.'

'Cor Cornflowery Cor I can do no more! Except grow & grow & put on a show, &, once again my flowers will be beautifully blue just for you.'

45

The story of Stork's Bill seed - via Springing & Drilling

'Where are you going Stork's Bill?' Asks Sunny.

'To find a home.'

'Where is home Stork's Bill?' Sunny questions.

'Wherever I fall but I could spring far because my spring is very well sprung.' Stork's Bill smiles because Stork's Bill has a very slick trick.

'Good luck Stork's Bill.' Says Sunny wondering why Stork's Bill is looking funny.'

47

'Welcome to your new home Stork's Bill.' Sunny says thrilled to see Stork's Bill has drilled & made a home all on its own.'

'Thank you Sunny. Do you know where I am?' Stork's Bill has to ask after the busy task.

'You are in open ground luckily for you with an armadillo for company dillying & dallying around with nothing better to do. Now you can grow & grow & make many more Stork's Bills to spring & drill & sow.'

'Storky stork! I drill for water because it is very dry & that is why. I am so clever, maybe I can live forever.'

The story of Cyclamen seed - via Ants

'Where are you going Cyclamen with your little parcels so bright & gay?' Asks Sunny.

'To seek a home.'

'Where is home Cyclamen?' Sunny asks.

'Wherever these little ants take me. It could be miles & miles away. I have a little present for them which is a treat, packed with things to eat. It will keep them going without slowing on their six little feet.'

'Good luck Cyclamen.' Says Sunny thinking the presents a slick trick & that the happy ants will take Cyclamen to a good place quick quick.

51

'Welcome to your new home Cyclamen. The ants have not treated you too well I see.' Said Sunny with sorrow noticing the ants have taken the presents & thrown Cyclamen out without a thought.

'Thank you Sunny but do not be sorry. The ants have only done what I want. Do you know where I am?' Says Cyclamen with a smile.

'You are on the ground with ant rubbish all around. I do think a thank you would have been nice even only said once & not twice.' Says Sunny not pleased.

'Hooray hooray what a day! I have given presents & been put out with the rubbish but I do not care a jot because I am just where I want to be.'

The story of All Sorts Of Seeds - via People

'Where are you going seeds in your millions & billions?' Sunny says with wonder.

'To find a home.' Came the loud reply.

'Where is home?' Said Sunny for once muddled & a bit befuddled.

'Wherever these people take us. Somewhere nice would suffice. By ship, lorry, plane, train & car, we have no fear whether it be near or perhaps far like a star.'

'Well good luck to you all.' Says Sunny, for once almost speechless.

'Welcome to your new homes.' Says Sunny amazed & dazed as well one might at such a sight.

'Thank you Sunny. Do you know where we are?'

'In fields in your millions & billions. Also in glass houses, gardens, nurseries & in lots of pots. See you around.' Sunny says feeling tired & it best to take a rest.

'Float, ride in the sky, twirl & swirl, be tasty, explode, shake rattle & roll, drop, grab, rumble & tumble, crawl & drill, present lots of presents! Never take being planted for granted. See you around Sunny. We are happy you are always there somewhere.'

Happy planting

Can you draw a line & match seed to plant?

Coconut seed

Dandelion seed

Sycamore seed

Strawberry seed

Sweet Pea seed

Poppy seed

Peanut seed

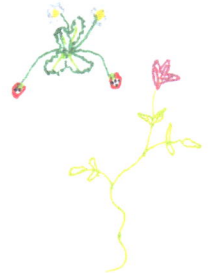

Hazelnut seed

Tumbleweed seed

Burdock seed

Cornflower seed

Stork's Bill seed

Cyclamen seed

All sorts of seeds

Lightning Source UK Ltd.
Milton Keynes UK
UKOW07f0628300417

300182UK00010B/53/P